POLICE CARS

LORI DITTMER

CREATIVE EDUCATION • CREATIVE PAPERBACKS

CONT

ENTS

I AM A POLICE CAR.

I patrol the roads.

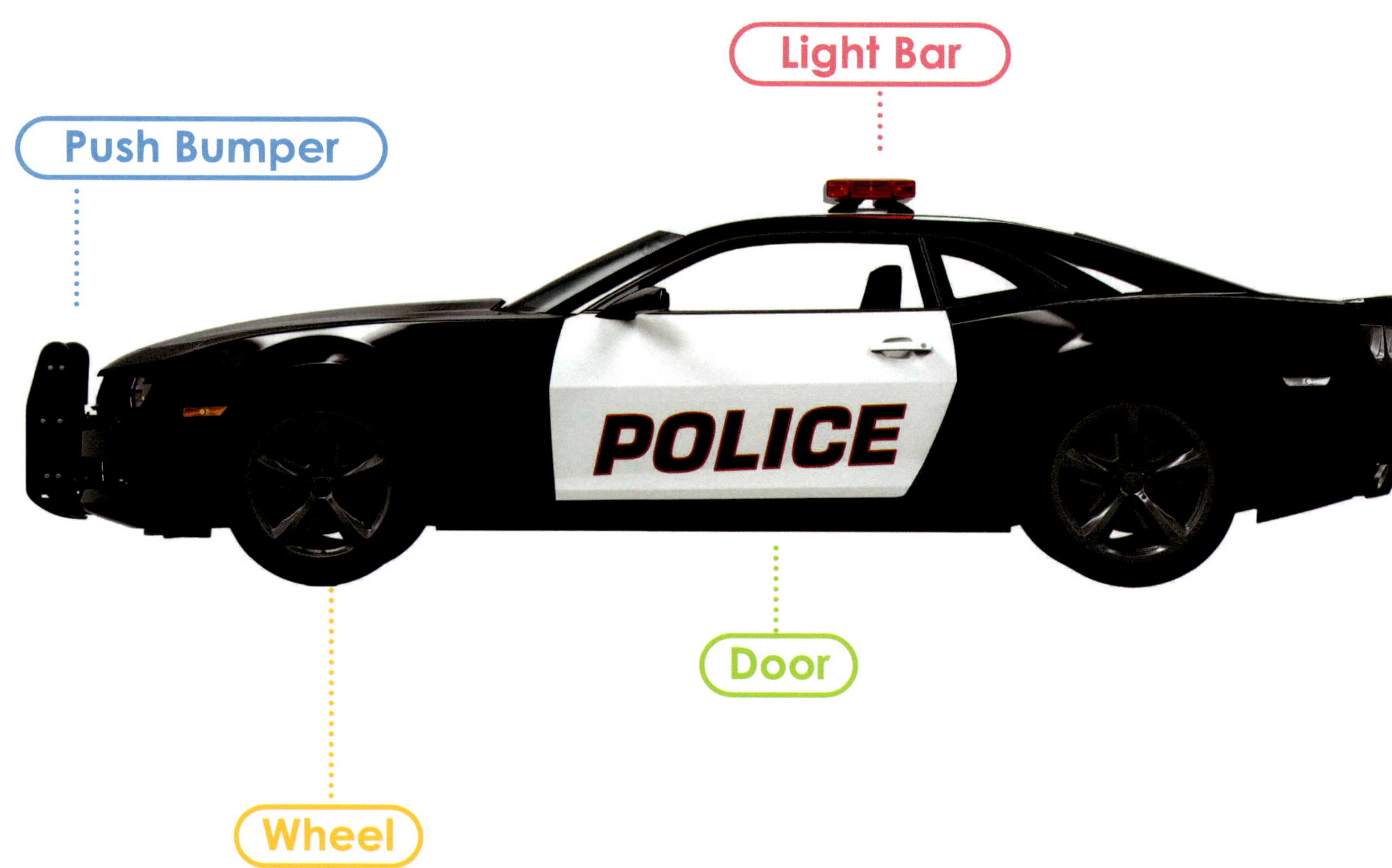

Look at
my light bar
and push
bumper!
POLICE

My black and white body is heavier than other cars.

A police officer drives. Sometimes another sits in front. They talk to other officers on the radio.

I race to help people.

My lights flash. They are red and blue.

My siren tells cars I am coming!

My engine
is powerful.

I can go 150 miles (241km) per hour! I drive on roads and bumpy ground.

I work hard to keep people safe.

MAKE A NOISE

Can you make a police car noise? They whoop, beep, and wail.

Listen to these sounds:

POLICE CARS WORDS

Engine: A machine that provides power and makes something move

Patrol: To keep watch over an area

Siren: Something that makes a long, loud sound as a warning

READING CORNER

Arnold, Quinn M. *Police Cars*. Mankato, Minn.: Creative Education and Creative Paperbacks, 2026.

Deniston, Natalie. *Police Cars*. Minneapolis: Jump!, 2026.

McDonald, Amy. *Police Cars*. Minneapolis: Bellwether Media, 2022.

PUBLISHED BY CREATIVE EDUCATION AND CREATIVE PAPERBACKS
P.O. Box 227, Mankato, Minnesota 56002
Creative Education and Creative Paperbacks are imprints of The Creative Company
www.thecreativecompany.us

COPYRIGHT © 2026 CREATIVE EDUCATION, CREATIVE PAPERBACKS
International copyright reserved in all countries. No part of this book may be reproduced in any form without written permission from the publisher.

LIBRARY OF CONGRESS CATALOGING-IN-PUBLICATION DATA
Names: Dittmer, Lori author
Title: Police cars / Lori Dittmer.
Description: Mankato, Minnesota : Creative Education and Creative Paperbacks, [2026] | Series: Starting out | Includes bibliographical references and index. | Audience: Ages 4-7 | Audience: Grades K-1 | Summary: "Introduce beginning readers to a day on the streets with a police car in this STEM starter. Includes photos, a labeled vehicle diagram, "Make a Noise" section, glossary, and further resources"— Provided by publisher.
Identifiers: LCCN 2025013151 (print) | LCCN 2025013152 (ebook) | ISBN 9798895810262 library binding | ISBN 9781682779798 paperback | ISBN 9798895811528 ebook
Subjects: LCSH: Police vehicles —Juvenile literature | CYAC: Police vehicles
Classification: LCC HV7936.V4 D58 2026 (print) | LCC HV7936.V4 (ebook) | DDC 629.20883632/32—dc23/eng/20250609
LC record available at https://lccn.loc.gov/2025013151
LC ebook record available at https://lccn.loc.gov/2025013152

DESIGN AND PRODUCTION
Design by Rhea Magaro
Art direction by Tom Morgan

PHOTOGRAPHS BY
Dreamstime/Frogtravel, 12, Nerthuz, 4, 14; Getty Images/halbergman, 5, Roy Morsch, 7; Microsoft Copilot, 10; Shutterstock/Like 3d Design, cover; Unsplash/Albert Stoynov, 2, Martin Jernberg, 11, Scott Rodgerson, 8, Tim Meyer, 6, Tom Morbey, 9

Every effort has been made to contact copyright holders for material reproduced in this book. Any omissions will be rectified in subsequent printings if notice is given to the publisher.

Printed in the United States